MW01717494

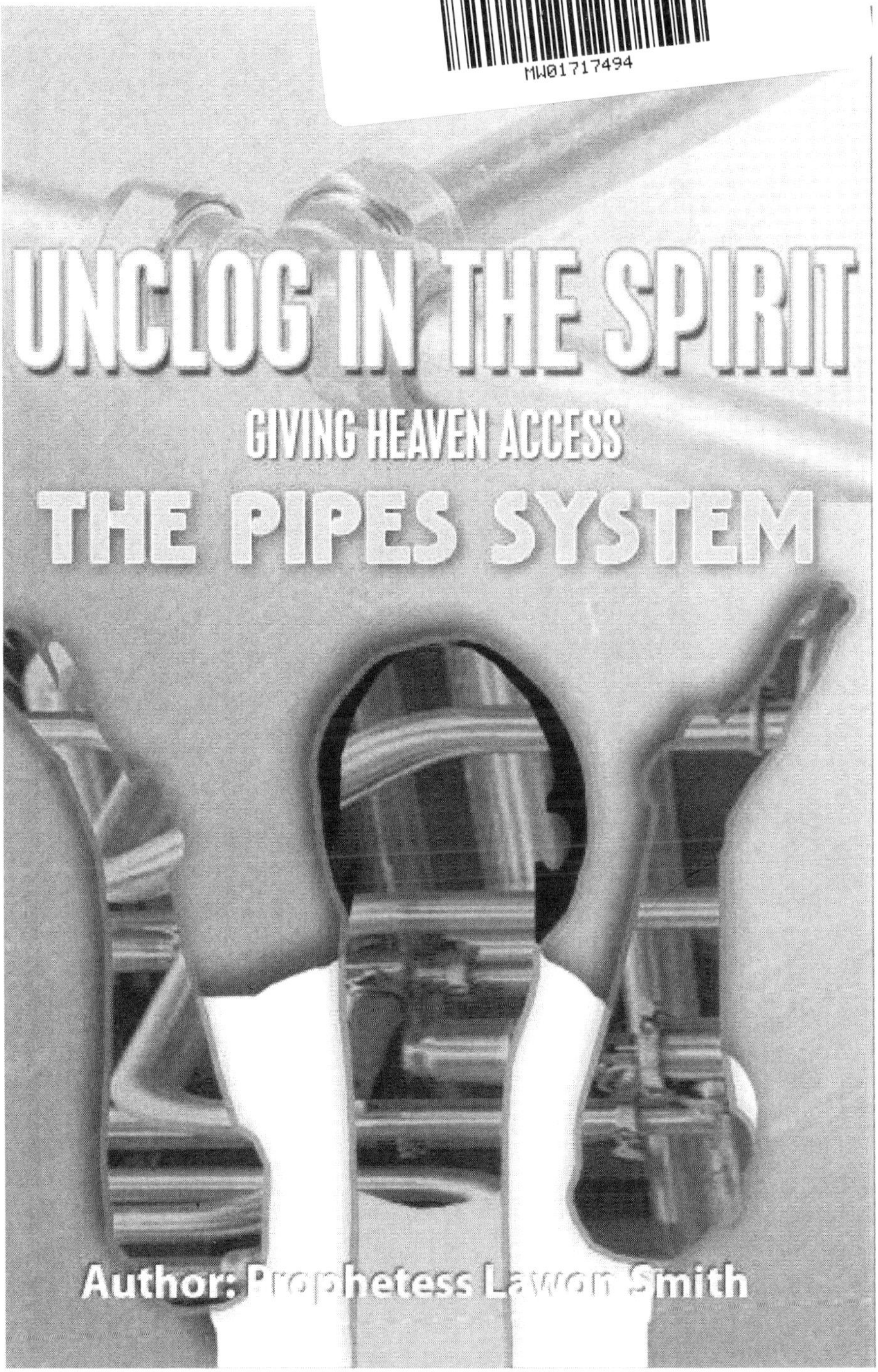
UNCLOG IN THE SPIRIT
GIVING HEAVEN ACCESS
THE PIPES SYSTEM
Author: Prophetess Lawon Smith

COPYRIGHT

Unclog In The Spirit: Giving Heaven Access – The Pipes System

All rights reserved. No part of this publication may be reproduced, stored in a retrieval system, or transmitted in any form or by any means-electronic, mechanical, photocopy, recording or any other-except brief quotations in printed reviews, without prior permission of the publisher. Unless otherwise indicated all verses are taken from The King James Version of the Bible. Definitions are from dictionary.com

Publisher: **Anointed Hands Publishing Company**
P.O. Box 438741
Chicago, Illinois 60643
www.ninamotivates.info
anointedhandspublishing@gmail.com

Copyright© 2017, by AH Publications, All rights reserved to Lawon Smith

ISBN: 9781513620121

THIS BOOK BELONGS TO

Kimberly

May the Lord
Speak peace to
your heart and
give you comfort
in His Presence

Love
Lauren

TABLE OF CONTENT

"Thy Kingdom come, thy will be done on Earth as it is in Heaven" (Matthew 6:10).

PIPES (**Prophetic Intercessory Prayer Enforcer Servant**) is a system of principles by which we allow the Holy Spirit to flow through us to get His will done on earth as it is in heaven.

"The will of God can flow through our nations, countries, cities, communities, churches and personal lives only when our spiritual systems are clear from of all the junk and clogs."

P ***–*** *Prophetic*

I *– Intercessory*

P *– Prayer*

E *– Enforcer*

S*-Servant*

Prophetic Intercessory Prayer Enforcer Servant's mission and purpose is to:

Lay ourselves down in a place of Prayer for the will of God to flow through us to the God intended places, people or times without any hindrances' in the way.

God communicates to the earth through those that will hear His voice.

This is not something new, but an awakening of the ministry that Jesus left for us on the earth, as He is in heaven yet interceding on our behalf. As Jesus intercedes for the believer it is the believer's responsibility to Pray for the activity of the world.

"Prayer is Love on its knees" The world needs prayer.

Introduction to the P.I.P.E.S Ministry

P.I.P.E.S Ministry was birthed through a personal experience with a toilet that would not flush in the house my family and I lived in for over ten years. We started Word of Truth in this house, so the toilet had a lot of customers. After being used by so many people we began to notice that the toilet was not flushing everything down in one jiggle of the handle. So we started to buy Drano to help unclog the pipes in the toilet and that would work for a while, then Drano stopped working. Then we started pouring water into the toilet to make sure everything would go down. Meanwhile we have three beautiful children that would use this same toilet but would sometimes forget about all the tricks we would have to perform to get the toilet to flush everything down. You are probably wondering what does this have to do with prayer. Just hold on to your tissues we are going somewhere.

At this point this toilet has made it the top of my prayer list, because prayer changes things right? Well, it did not change that toilet, but it began to change me. Scripture's came to me like, "out of your belly shall flow rivers of living water" (John 7:38). "Let thy Kingdom come and thy will be done on earth as it is in the heavens" (Matt. 6:10). "Well spring forth oh wells of Jacob. I am the living water" (John 4:14 NIV). Along with people saying it is wrong to question God; I say He has the answer to every question one could ask.

He will answer your questions but it may not be what you want to hear. The Lord showed me that as a prophet with the ministry of intercession, I give him access to move in the earth as he had when Jesus walked the earth. Everything needs a system to flow through in the natural as well as in the spirit. For example, Mary's system was used by God to Flow the Son of God to the earth.

As you read this manual be refreshed, reproved, restored, rebuked and redeemed. Most of all my desire is that you will yield to the cleansing of the Holy Spirit, be liberated in your prayer life and receive the Love of God in His chambers. Enjoy this journey of totally surrendering to the Lord. Take one last look at the mess and flush the toilet for real.

Prophetess Lawon Smith

Chapter 1 Getting the Blue Print

"Understanding God's Plan"

God is a Master Architect, however, he does not work without a Blueprint. The blueprint gives you information on how to build what should be visibly seen. Blueprints are also known as a detailed outline or a plan of action and used to form a strategy for a project. We can see God using this pattern when he gave Noah instructions or a blueprint for the Ark. Moses received a blueprint for the Tabernacle. King David was also given the instructions to rebuild the Tabernacle and because of the blood on his hand, his son had to follow the pattern to build the temple. Even the Apostles of the early church in the New Testament were given a blueprint for the Kingdom.

The goal is Matthews 6:10 "Your kingdom come. Your will be done on earth as it is in heaven (KJV)." In order His will to be done on earth as it is in heaven, the crew meaning the saints, must know how to read the blueprints from heaven. Before an architect starts a project he has already spent time going over the plans and getting an understanding of what is needed and necessary to get the project accomplished. Gods' Kingdom is what needs to be visibly seen in the earth, but His will is the blueprint on how to make His Kingdom visible.

We have learned to pray the model of these instructions, but God is causing the intercessors and other leaders to erect an image of heaven in the earth that would cause the earth to seek this Kingdom. "Nevertheless we, according to His promise, look for new heavens and a new earth in which righteousness dwells" (2 Peter 3:12-14 KJV).

Even though we have an idea based on what the book of Revelations say about what heaven looks like. It is important for the unbeliever to have an opportunity to encounter this Kingdom before leaving the earth. The question is how can this be done?

Through our righteousness is this kingdom manifested to the unbelievers. "For the kingdom of God is not in eating and drinking, but righteousness and peace and joy in the Holy Spirit" (Romans 14:17 KJV). We will touch on the importance of the Holy Spirit in our lifestyle of prayer in chapter 8. After the blueprints are designed the Architect has to put together a team to accomplish the project. He needs a welder, concert specialist, Foreman, forklift driver, brick layer and many other team players. The Architect has to think about the team from the inside as well as the outside of a building. We would not want to have a nice structure on the outside and the inside has no walls, stairs or elevators to get to the floors in the building.

God is putting together a team for His kingdom, but there are some qualities the members should have in order to be a part of the project. After all blueprints have no value if you do not have anyone working on the plan of action. Without people, the blue prints are just a piece of paper, but when people connect with the blueprints, things begin to happen. The vision begins to come to life.

"Where there is no vision, the people perish" (Proverbs 29:18 KJV). "Where there is no revelation, the people cast off restraint" (Proverbs 29:18 NKJV).

When we take the time to spend with the Lord, He reveals His (vision, revelation or blueprint) plans to us. You may be wondering what you are called to do in His Kingdom. What is your role or position? The only way that your assignment will be revealed is through asking (praying) to God. Perish means to suffer destruction or ruin. When we do not have the blueprint according to the word we suffer destruction. The revealed plan of God causes us to have self-control. Restraint means to be hindered, limited freedom. Understanding the plan gives us protection from the plans of the enemy. "If people can't see what God is doing, they stumble all over themselves" (Proverbs 29:18 Message).

This is a good place to reflect. Answer the question below:

1. Do I know what God's' plan is for my personal life? Please give some detail with your answer.

2. Am I a part of a team? What is my team building and why?

3. Write the scriptures used in this chapter.

"The secret of seeking is not in our human ascent to God, but in Gods descent to us. We start out searching, but we end up being discovered. We think we are looking for something; we realize we are found by someone. As in the Francis Thompson's famous picture, 'the hound of heaven' has tracked us down. What brings us home is not our discovery of the way home but the call of the Father who has been waiting there for us all along, whose presence there makes home, home."

–Os Guinness (Guinness, 1998)

Chapter 2

Breaking Ground

"Allow God into your Heart"

The desire to pray was birthed out of a broken place in my life. I cannot keep up with the number of times that I found myself up in the middle of the night with a pillow soaked with tears of despair and loneliness. While my Ex-husband laid next me sound asleep. Part of me was angry with him because I felt like he should be up comforting me, but the truth of matter was, I had to connect with God. "The Lord is nigh unto them that are of a broken heart; and saveth such as of a contrite spirit" (Psalm 34:18 KJV). "If your heart is broken, you'll find God right there; if you're kicked in the gut, he'll help you catch your breath" (Psalm 34:18 MSG). It is important to not allow the emotional pain that we may experience be dependent on man for the answer. God is drawn to the tears of His people. When our hearts have been infected by life God desires to be the cure.

This is where we lose a lot of intercessors, because dealing with the heart takes work naturally and spiritually. "Keep thy heart with all diligence; for out of it are the issues of life" (Proverbs 4:23 KJV). To keep something means one would need to know and understand the value of what needs to be kept. If we understood the value of keeping our bodies there would be fewer children born out of wedlock. God wants our whole heart because where our hearts are is where our desires and treasures are stored. In the natural the heart is the source of life, once the heart stops beating oftentimes the person is declared dead. Spiritually, if our hearts are not beating for the Lord the believer is dead in faith. When we give God access to our heart we receive life. An intercessor must know what their source of life is in order to be effective during prayer.

"If I regard iniquity in my heart, the Lord will not hear me" (Psalm 66:18 KJV). According to the dictionary iniquity means lack of justice or righteousness; wickedness; a wicked act; sin. No one wants to deal with sin when they think they are saved, but the truth is that we all have sinned and fell short of His Glory (Romans

3:23 KJV). When we carry offenses (un-forgiveness) against people we hinder God from hearing what we pray.

If we pray all night and have iniquity in our heart the principle will not change. Iniquity also hinders us from seeing God (Matthew 5:8 KJV). According to Isaiah 32:6, iniquity in our hearts can and will affect our speech. The purpose of highlighting this is because most of you reading this manual have already had some kind of encounter with God and now have a desire to go deeper. Before this can be achieved the iniquity in the heart has to be exposed and dealt with through prayer and deliverance.

PIPES Ministries is about an individual laying down his/her life in a place that is not comfortable, choosing to be purged from self, and positioned for God to flow through them. To get His heart, mind and will to the ordained people, place and situations that He desires. The heart is where the "flow from heaven" begins, and if the heart is full of iniquity then what we receive from heaven will be contaminated with the hidden sin and wickedness in our heart. "This people draweth nigh unto me with their mouth, and honoureth me with their lips; but their heart is far from me" (Matthew 15:8 KJV). Don't go to the grave with prayers being hindered because of un-repented sin. It is time to stop lying to ourselves saying that we are ok when clearly we are not. Before we can pray for others, we have to be honest about our need for deliverance.

The work of repentance is the intercessor's greatest weapon because it puts everyone back into their proper place. When we repent it makes us turn from ourselves, arrest the devil and puts God on the throne of our hearts. Writing this chapter challenged me to deal with things in my heart that I did not realize was hindering God from hearing my prayers. It is important to be honest and repent from dead works of the flesh, and also church work. Church work is necessary for the work of the ministry, but it means nothing if our hearts are full of unrighteousness, bitterness, un-forgiveness, strife, envy, malice, selfishness, lust and hatred; just to name a few. Psalm 51 is the perfect tool to use before entering into prayer on the behalf of others.

David cried from his heart about his heart because he knew that his heart was not like God's. Until we have arrived at the gates we are not exempt from having our hearts filled with iniquity. We must humble ourselves and understand that we need the mercy of God just like everyone that we pray for in this lifetime. An intercessor needs to desire truth in the inward parts of the heart. The heart unchecked can cause us to deceive ourselves (Jeremiah 17:9 KJV). This is why God tells us to give our heart back to Him because He knows the heart better than we do (Psalm 44:21). There is so much more that can be shared about allowing God in our heart but we will stop right here and take some time to search our hearts with the Word and allow the Holy Spirit to show us what is not like God.

Psalm 51

King James Version (KJV)

1 Have mercy upon me, O God, according to thy lovingkindness: according unto the multitude of thy tender mercies blot out my transgressions.
2 Wash me throughly from mine iniquity, and cleanse me from my

sin. [3]For I acknowledge my transgressions: and my sin is
ever before me. [4]Against thee, thee only, have I sinned,
and done this evil in thy sight: that thou mightest be
justified when thou speakest, and be clear when thou
judgest. [5]Behold, I was shapen in iniquity; and in sin did
my mother conceive me. [6]Behold, thou desirest truth in
the inward parts: and in the hidden part thou shalt make
me to know wisdom. [7]Purge me with hyssop, and I shall
be clean: wash me, and I shall be whiter than
snow. [8]Make me to hear joy and gladness; that the
bones which thou hast broken may rejoice. [9]Hide thy
face from my sins, and blot out all mine
iniquities. [10]Create in me a clean heart, O God; and
renew a right spirit within me. [11]Cast me not away from
thy presence; and take not thy holy spirit from
me. [12]Restore unto me the joy of thy salvation; and
uphold me with thy free spirit. [13]Then will I teach
transgressors thy ways; and sinners shall be converted
unto thee. [14]Deliver me from bloodguiltiness, O God,
thou God of my salvation: and my tongue shall sing
aloud of thy righteousness. [15]O Lord, open thou my lips;
and my mouth shall shew forth thy praise. [16]For thou

desirest not sacrifice; else would I give it: thou delightest
not in burnt offering. [17]The sacrifices of God are a
broken spirit: a broken and a contrite heart, O God, thou
wilt not despise. [18]Do good in thy good pleasure unto
Zion: build thou the walls of Jerusalem. [19]Then shalt
thou be pleased with the sacrifices of righteousness,
with burnt offering and whole burnt offering: then shall
they offer bullocks upon thine altar.

Reflection:

1. What is the condition of your heart at this present time?

____

____

____

____

____

____

2. What part of this lesson has caused you to make some changes? Why?

____

____

____

____

____

____

3. What are you willing to do to live a life of prayer?

____

____

____

____

____

____

"The greatest privilege of prayer is that of coming into the actual presence of God to enjoy loving conversation and communion with Him. We are to pray frequently (1 Thessalonians 5:17) and openly (Revelation 3:20) and even 'with confidence so that we may receive mercy and find grace to help us in our time of need' (Hebrews 4:16). What an invitation! There is non another like it."

–Paul Cedar

Chapter 3 Prophetic

"Seeing, Hearing, Speaking and Praying what God Reveals"

Prayer is a communication between us and God. The prophetic allows us to be open to how God will communicate to us. "Surely the Lord God will do nothing, but he revealeth his secret unto his servants the prophets" (Amos 3:7). We do not have to occupy the office of a prophet for God to communicate to us. The word prophets in this scripture mean: *nabiy (naw-bee). According to the Strong's Concordance nabiy (naw-bee) is an inspired people.* God will not do anything in the earth without having an inspired people to partner with Him in the earth. Abraham was a prophet that God communicated His plan to when he wanted to destroy Sodom. We are the seeds of Abraham with the same access to the counsel, mind, heart and will of the Father. Jesus is always a great example of the prophetic being released in the earth through a human being. When Jesus walked the earth He always revealed what the Father's plans were for the earth and His purpose in fulfilling God's will through him. "At that time Jesus answered and said, I thank thee, O Father, Lord of heaven and earth, because thou hast hid these things from the wise and prudent, and hast revealed them unto babes" (Matthew 11:25 KJV).

The prophetic dimension as it relates to prayer and intercession takes us beyond the long list that we may have written out and our five senses. Prayer is a spiritual work done by spiritual people that should be inspired by the God they are praying to. "But if they be prophets (inspired people), and if the word of the Lord be with them, let them now make intercession to the Lord of hosts, that the vessels which are left in the house of the Lord, and in the house of the king of Judah, and at Jerusalem, go not to Babylon" (Jeremiah 27:18 KJV). Intercessors are the ones in the church that will more than likely see the chaos, hear the confusion and demonic attacks that can take place within a gathering. Prophetic intercession allows the intercessor to speak into the atmosphere God's will through prayer. Oftentimes intercessors can fall into complaining when they see and hear other things that do not line up with the word of God. This is strongly discouraged because God is allowing us to see and hear only to partner with Him so that the outcome can change. God challenge the saints in Jeremiah to make intercession so that the people that were in the house of God would not be given over to Babylon.

There will be times in prayer that we will not know what to pray or how to pray.

Romans 8:26-27

King James Version (KJV)

26 Likewise the Spirit also helpeth our infirmities: for we know not what we should pray for as we ought: but the Spirit itself maketh intercession for us with groanings which cannot be uttered. 27 And he that searcheth the hearts knoweth what is the mind of the Spirit, because he maketh intercession for the saints according to the will of God.

Romans 8:26-27

The Message (MSG)

[26-28]Meanwhile, the moment we get tired in the waiting, God's Spirit is right alongside helping us along. If we don't know how or what to pray, it doesn't matter. He does our praying in and for us, making prayer out of our wordless sighs, our aching groans. He knows us far better than we know ourselves, knows our pregnant condition, and keeps us present before God. That's why we can be so sure that every detail in our lives of love for God is worked into something good.

According to the Message Romans 8:26-27 tells us that God knows that we have the ability to birth out His will when we pray. What an honor to be pregnant with the perfect will of God and then have the ability to see the manifestation of what God has revealed. Hannah had no idea why she was barren; the scriptures revealed that the Lord had shut up her womb. Something so mind blowing happened when she began to cry out to the Lord in the temple. God released productivity into her spirit and womb. Hannah brought forth the Prophet Samuel, what is in us waiting to be released from the Spirit? Have we become desperate enough to cry out to release the heart of God into the earth? These are just a few questions to start the process of seeking God for his perfect will when we pray. When God reveals his will we should be in position to receive it and then pray it!

Reflection:

1. What does the word prophetic mean?

2. How does the prophetic benefit us in prayer?

3. Give an example from the bible of prophetic intercession? Do not use what is in the manual!

"When we know the depth of our need For God and when we are convinced that God's purpose is far superior to our preference, then we are ready to yield to God and to do God's will. 'Your will be done' is a prayer that God will bridle us and direct us, wherever that may lead." –Brain J Dodd

Chapter 4 Intercessory

"On behalf of Another"

Sometimes because there is such a comfort in the presence of God we can forget about others and just talk to God about me, myself and I. Intercession is the work that we commit to on the behalf of another. The word Intercession means to:

- Huperentugchano to intercede for one intercession
- Entugchano to light upon a person or a thing, fall in with, hit upon, a person or a thing to go to or meet a person, esp. for the purpose of conversation, consultation, or supplication to pray, entreat make intercession for any one.
- Bela` Bela = "destruction" n pr m a king of Edom first son of Benjamin a son of Ahaz, a Reubenite n pr loc one of the five cities of the plain which was

spared at the intercession of Lot, and received the name of Zoar

- Paga` to encounter, meet, reach, entreat, make intercession (Qal) to meet, light upon, join to meet (of kindness) to encounter, fall upon (of hostility) to encounter, entreat (of request) to strike, touch (of boundary) (Hiphil) to cause to light upon to cause to entreat to make entreaty, interpose to make attack to reach the mark

The work of intercession is selfless and calls us into a covenant relationship with the Lord. The definitions given are key in helping us go deeper in our understanding. **Paga** stands out for the purpose of this lesson because it gives a more intense meaning of the word intercession. Intercession takes an encounter with God that will cause a person to confront the devil and reach in with the word to change a situation. When you have been made aware of the dangers or events that can cause destruction to a person or a region you should have a response of intercession. Sometimes we can become desensitized to the press on our heart or spirit as it relates to praying for others.

Abraham was made aware of the sins of Sodom and Gomorrah, even though God said he want to destroy them Abraham's response was to petition for mercy. An intercessor or one interceding should respond in the spirit to spiritual matters. The scripture shows us how God illuminated (to cause to light upon) His plan to Abraham. In return, Abraham entreated God, and brought His will to His remembrance to spare the city from destruction and to save his family. However, after pleading abundantly with God, he realized that the people in the city did not even want to be saved, but God did spare Abraham's family from this judgement. We can model this same response today in our life.

God is going to judge the sins of the world, but the intercessor will be able to be a part of the process. Jesus is our greatest example of an intercessor. He walked in the physical on earth interfering with the plan of the devil. Jesus is still in position as an intercessor on our behalf while He is in heaven. Let's think about the fact that He (Jesus) went to jail, was convicted, carried his cross, was beaten along the way, nailed to the cross, died, was buried, resurrected, ascended and still yet makes intercession on our behalf. Protect your position as an intercessor, someone's life is dependent on our commitment to prayer. God is depending on us just as he did Jesus in the earth, to occupy the position of intercession.

Reflection:

1. What does it mean to intercede?

____

____

____

____

____

____

2. Have you ever stood between God and a person like Abraham? Share in detail.

____

____

____

____

____

____

____

3. How will you move forward after reading this chapter on intercession?

____

____

____

____

____

"By the same work of the Spirit within us, I believe we can learn to look beyond our personal situation to those around us- our families, our communities, our nation, and our world. God will instill His concern for others within our hearts so that we can start to care for them as He does. Our prayers for them begin to flow more readily. We yearn for others to receive their salvation from His hand, to know his tender care as their Father and Friend." –Shirley Dobson

Chapter 5 Prayer

"How to use the Word when engaged in Prayer"

No one desires to spend time talking to someone that doesn't respond back. The importance of getting your prayers answered is understanding how to partner with scriptures during your time of prayer. We will discover how to identify the problem and pray the solution. Practice in prayer what God said. The objective of this chapter is to also understand that partnership with scriptures is what sets Christians apart from other religions that practice prayer. We pray in Jesus name. Jesus is still interceding for us not like other deities that others may pray to. Understanding that He has given us permission to use His name should give us a new perspective in the way we approach prayer.

I had walked into a store and as I began to look for the items I came in the store for, I heard a disturbing sound. It was a three year old little boy upset and crying, the other kids was looking trying figure out what his problem was, and the mom was frustrated. I turned the corner and interrupted the little boy. He stopped and looked at me as if to say 'who do you think you are interrupting my temper tantrum.' While he was calm I gently said, "Use your words, and tell me what's wrong so we can fix it." At this point it felt like the store had stopped and everyone's eye were and me and this little boy. He just wanted to be picked up because he was exhausted from walking. The mother was just shocked that I was able to calm the little boy and how he just started talking to me. Please, don't have temper tantrums in prayer, use the Word of God. This does not mean that we cannot be emotional in prayer, it just means that we should grow in prayer from the grocery list into a more focused and effective use of the time we spend in prayer each time.

"My people are destroyed for lack of knowledge: because thou hast rejected knowledge, I will also reject thee, that thou shalt be no priest to me: seeing thou hast forgotten the law of ***thy*** *God, I will also forget thy children" (Hosea 4:6 KJV).*

We are ineffective in the place of prayer when we lack knowledge of God's Word. This is where we become challenged because of the call to discipline. Most officers are trained and disciplined. Even the superhero takes the time to know or get knowledge of their strengths and weaknesses. When we don't know the law, we open the door to ignorance and death. We are destroyed according to the scripture for a lack of knowledge. We must possess knowledge of good and evil, God and the devil, a balanced perspective gives us the advantage to stand in the fight. A person that knows they will win a fight is the least likely to quit.

We have confidence in the God of the bible, in Isaiah 55:11, He personally sent His word (Jesus) with a guarantee that it will produce fruit:

"It is the same with my word. I send it out, and it always produces fruit. It will accomplish all I want it to, and it will prosper everywhere I send it." Isaiah 55:11 NLT

"But when ye pray, use not vain repetitions, as the heathen do: for they think that they shall be heard for their much speaking" (Matthew 6:7 KJVS).

Write a Prayer using a scripture that in this Chapter or what Holy Spirit speaks to you as you pray.

Chapter 6 Enforcer

"Not letting go until God say So!"

"From the days of John the Baptist until now the kingdom of heaven suffers violent assault, and violent men seize it by force [as a precious prize]" (MATTHEW 11:12 AMP).

Super heroes will always win the fight against evil because that's the way it was written and so it is with us as believers. When we rise to the occasion to be an enforcer of God's will we win. The beautiful thing about enforcing God's will is that we win on the behalf of others. What is an enforcer? According to the dictionary an Enforcer is a group or person that compels observations or compliance with a law, rule or obligation a person who imposes their will by violence and intimidation. A police officer is one in the natural that enforces laws, regulations and rules set by the government. When we become an enforcer in the earth for the kingdom of God, we must know the law.

We must exercise the authority given to us by God. Not towards people, but in the spirit and there will be time you will confront people with these spirits that oppose the law of God. John the Baptist was known because he openly rebuked all those that were in sin. He called them to repentance. We must, as believers, enforce God's laws in our own lives first. Heroes can fall into the mode of saving others before they consider them self. The best way to stay humble is to first examine your own life, seeking the area that you can enforce the will of God in your life. No one respects that dirty cop that has their hands in the same dirt as the ones they take to jail! We can't expect God to give us the authority over the devil that we dance with.

Taking responsibility for the position and title that you may carry. We are ambassadors for the kingdom of God with access to heaven on earth. God has anointed us by faith. Which means He trust us to be His voice in the earth. We should not abuse the authority that God has given us as enforcers. Just because you have the right, it is important to still operate in compassion. Super heroes have extraordinary powers that can protect as well as hurt people. What makes them a hero is that they have decided to protect people from the forces of darkness.

Enforcers must have knowledge of spiritual warfare in the fight against good and evil. Jesus was aware of the devil's plan for humanity so he decided to become the sacrifice that would stand against the plans of the devil and bring deliverance. Enforcers bring deliverance, through prayer and casting out devils. We have to believe and have faith that people want to be free. Our fight is not against flesh and blood. We will give up if we fight based on the flesh because it may appear that people don't want to save. No one wants to fight for the person that does not fight from themselves. This thought is carnal. However the scripture reminds us that "how can they see when the god of this world has blinded their eyes." 2 Corinthians chapter 4 is worth reading in order to understand this principal.

List words that mean to not let go

What was one thing you will use from the chapter?

What your name as a superhero and why?

Chapter 7 Servant

"He reveals the secret things to His Servants"

Intercession is a service from the earth to the heavens. We are servants in prayer. God told Abram about what His plan was for Sodom and Gomorrah. Abraham didn't go run and tell Lot what thus saith the Lord like a prophet. Abraham the role of a servant on the behalf of Lot through prayer to interfere with the death of him and his family. In this chapter, we must transform our attitude towards people and prayer. Servants don't get to select who they serve that is God's job. We have been employed by the creator of the universe to get a job done in the earth according to Matthew 6:10.

Genesis 13 is when Abraham decides to give Lot the opportunity to go into another part of the land for the sake of peace. Lot chose to go near Sodom where the land appeared to better and Abraham took the other side. Abraham could have had an attitude with Lot about his decision, but he blessed him and his family. In

Genesis 14 a war between kings break out in the land, Lot was captured and word gets to Abraham. Abraham could have decided not to get involved with this war, but the intercessor (interceptor) was born to intervene on the behalf of another.

There will be times that we must fight for others, even if what's taking place does not directly affect us. Abraham positioned himself in between God, the enemy and Lot.

Three plans at work which one will produce an outcome that will bring Glory to God. The servant of the Lord couldn't resist the opportunity to make God name great. Abraham didn't make this moment about him, he stayed focused on the end results. Servants can't afford to get personally caught up in the emotion of a moment and miss the opportunity to bring Glory to the name of God on the behalf of another.

A servant has to be trusted in order to handle secrets. When God reveals something to a prophet, God expects you to wait. Example of this would be Sarah. She was told she would give birth to a child, but she decides to do it her way because she didn't wait on the promise. Just because we hear a Word from God doesn't mean we have the permission to just move about. A good server will repeat the order back to the person they are waiting on. Then they may ask is there anything you want to add to this order, and then they inform them that their order will be given to the cook.

Process is important, when developing as an intercessor and prophet. By now we should have grown in our understanding about prayer, prophetic and intercession. Now we can move into action. The next chapter on obedience will help to access the power we need as a believer.

1. What is the definition of a servant? Give a parallel of a servant and intercessor.

2. Why is it important to wait?

3. What will you do differently after reading this chapter?

Chapter 8 Obedience

"Responding to the Leading of the Holy Spirit"

I spent a lot of time thinking that it was about waking up at 5 am every morning and praying, over time I learned that it was about obedience. You can wake up at the same time every day to pray and not be obedient. Discipline and obedience are two different concepts. In this chapter, we will explore the difference, but understand that both are important. Our disobedience in prayer can affect others. We will learn how to break free from rebellion for the sake of others. The Holy Spirit has a part to play in the area of obedience. We seek to understand how to better partner with the Holy Spirit in prayer.

The definition of discipline is training to act in accordance with rules, drills, punishment inflicted by way of correction and training. Also activity, exercise, or a regimen that develops or improves a skill, defines discipline. When we are called to the place of prayer or operate in the prophetic we must be disciplined. When

Jesus came to the earth he started off as a baby so we know that he had to develop discipline in order to carry out his assignment in the earth. We cannot bypass discipline and expect to function in obedience consistently. Most of the time we deal with being disciplined by focusing on the punishment inflicted. By way of definition we see that discipline involves training and we don't want to take the time to develop habits or behavior due to the fear to being punished. We want to renew our mind about discipline so we can become effective intercessors for the glory of God.

This chapter should have been the first because when I was writing this chapter I was walking out the obedience factor. I thought that I was obedient, but I learned that there are levels in obedience just like faith. God will push you into those uncomfortable, unfamiliar places to produce the manifestation of the greatness that already is on the inside of us. It was like a fight with self, the devil and Holy Spirit. Getting up early in the morning, the voices in my head saying 'get up', 'no just lay down you are tired', 'the time is now and if you don't get up you will miss God.' The struggle was real, but God was and will always began doing something when we are at the end of ourselves.

We are going to always be at the end of a thing only to experience the beginning of a thing. You are probably just as confused as I was going through the development of allowing the Holy Spirit to lead. The fact of the matter is knowing the Holy Spirit's role, responsibility, character and desire can teach you how to obey. Once you make the decision to give yourself to a life of prayer and intercession you will understand what I am trying to give to you through this manual.

Now that you are at the end of this manual, please take some time to journal your journey. What were your thoughts when you started and what are your thoughts now? In addition, Write down some declarations and confessions that will help fortify your prayer life.

Bibliography/Reference

All quotations have been adapted from the material below:

Ridings, D. (2003). *Pray!* Colorado Springs: NavPress.

Os Guinness, The Call (Nashville; Word Publishing 1998) p.14

Paul Cedar, A Life of Prayer (Nashville, TN: Word Publishing 1998), p.16

Brain J. Dodd, Pray Jesus Way (Downers Grove IL; Intervarsity Press, 1997) p. 77

Shirley Dobson, Certain Peace in Uncertain Times (Sisters, or: Multnomah Publisher, Inc, 2002) p.43

PROPHETESS LAWON SMITH

Prophetess Lawon Smith is the Director and Mother of PIPES Ministries (Prophetic, Intercessory, Prayer, Enforcer, Servants), an ordained prophet, doula, consultant and program director. PIPES Ministries aids, assist and activates others in spiritual gifts for the perfecting of the Body of Christ (Ephesians 4:11-3). Prophetess Lawon has trained and developed others in intercession and the prophetic, in order to strengthen local churches. She is passionate about prayer and the Word (Matthew 6:9). She is a true Mother in Zion with a heart to labor with women of all nations. Prophetess Lawon is the mother of three beautiful children (Antione, Antionette and Ajay), a new grandmother and a host of spiritual children. She is the Board Chair of "You Can Make It" women and children shelter. She has worked with women for over 18 years spiritually and naturally through conferences, retreats, workshops and one-on-one discipleship.

Prophetess Lawon holds a degree in Not for Profit Management from North Park University, currently pursuing A Masters in Theology and a Case Manager at DuPage County working with the Elderly. She was the director of Word of Truth Outreach a full service food pantry that feed over a 1000 families for many years. She is passionate about helping people spiritual and naturally. She has housed families in her own home that have gone on to be very successful in life. Hard working, dedicated, loving, strong and inspiring are just a few words that describe this lady. She has overcome incest, rape, abandonment, rejection, insanity, death, depression, divorce, hurt, just to name a few. However, if there was only one word to describe Prophetess Lawon true nature it would be balanced, in the midst of all of her tragedies, traumatic events, accomplishments and responsibilities she knows that a balanced woman is a Kingdom Woman. She only desires to bring God Glory in and through whatever she do in this life.

Contact us for classes to help develop a house of prayer, activate the prophetic, and strengthen intercessors and personal growth in the spirit. Also for workshops, speaking engagements or Books.

Prophetess Lawon A Smith

Email: pipes62009@gmail.com

Office: 334-610-1860

Website: www.pipesunrestrictedprayer.webs.com